weblinks

You don't need a computer to use this book. But, for readers who do have access to the Internet, the book provides links to recommended websites which offer additional information and resources on the subject.

You will find weblinks boxes like this on some pages of the book.

> ## weblinks
> For more information about training and teaching, go to www.waylinks.co.uk/series/soyouwant/children

waylinks.co.uk

To help you find the recommended websites easily and quickly, weblinks are provided on our own website, **waylinks.co.uk.** These take you straight to the relevant websites and save you typing in the Internet address yourself.

Internet safety

➶ Never give out personal details, which include: your name, address, school, telephone number, email address, password and mobile number.

➶ Do not respond to messages which make you feel uncomfortable – tell an adult.

➶ Do not arrange to meet in person someone you have met on the Internet.

➶ Never send your picture or anything else to an online friend without a parent's or teacher's permission.

➶ If you see anything that worries you, tell an adult.

A note to adults
Internet use by children should be supervised. We recommend that you install filtering software which blocks unsuitable material.

Website content

The weblinks for this book are checked and updated regularly. However, because of the nature of the Internet, the content of a website may change at any time, or a website may close down without notice. While the Publishers regret any inconvenience this may cause readers, they cannot be responsible for the content of any website other than their own.

HODDER
Wayland

So You Want To Work With

Children?

Margaret McAlpine

HODDER
Wayland

an imprint of Hodder Children's Books

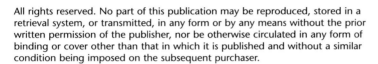

First published in 2004 by Hodder Wayland,
an imprint of Hodder Children's Books

© Hodder Wayland 2003

Editor: Laura Milne
Inside design: Peta Morey
Cover design: Hodder Wayland

British Library Cataloguing Publication Data
McAlpine, Margaret
So you want to work with children?
1.Child care – Vocational guidance – Juvenile literature
2.Social work with children – Vocational guidance – Juvenile literature
I.Title
362.7'023

ISBN 0 7502 4529 8

Printed in China by WKT Company Ltd.

Hodder Children's Books
A division of Hodder Headline Limited
338 Euston Road, London NW1 3BH

Picture Acknowledgements. The publishers would like to thank the following
for allowing their pictures to be reproduced in this publication:
Jonathan Cavendish/Corbis 19b; Corbis 20, 22, 29, 34, 37, 39, 43l, 51 (both),
53, 54, 57, 59b; Jim Craigmyle/Corbis 43r; Laura Dwight/Corbis 15; Ed Bock
Photography Inc./Corbis 16, 30, 45, 48, 59t; D. Robert Franz/Corbis 5;
Gaetano/Corbis 7; Patrik Giardino/Corbis 17; Ken Glaser/Corbis 9; Tom
Grill/Corbis 4, 11r, 13; Walter Hodges/Corbis 32; Jeff Zaruba Studio/Corbis
19t; JFPI Studios Inc./Corbis 12, 27t; John Henley Photography/Corbis 40, 46;
Jose Luis Pelaez Inc./Corbis 24, 25, 31, 35; Jutta Klee/Corbis 23; Larry Williams
and Associates/Corbis 27b, 28, 33, 49; Kevin R. Morris/Corbis 8; Jules
Perrier/Corbis 6; Steve Prezant/Corbis 41; Rob Lewine Photography/Corbis 52;
Joel Sartore/Corbis 11l; Ariel Skelley/Corbis 44, 47; Tom Stewart
Photography/Corbis 14, 21, 36, 38, 55, 56.

Note: Photographs illustrating the 'day in the life of' pages are posed
by models.

Contents

Words in **bold** can be found in the glossary.

Nursery Nurse

What is a nursery nurse?

Nursery nurses look after young children, usually before they are old enough to go to school, but sometimes until they are up to eight years old. It is the job of a nursery nurse to keep children safe and happy and to help them to develop the different skills they will need to cope with life as they grow older.

They work in many different places including **nurseries**, **day care centres**, **play centres** and hospitals. They may also work in private homes, looking after children while their parents or carers go out to work, or are away from home.

Some hotels, sports centres, shopping centres, factories and offices have **crèches** where parents/carers can leave their children knowing they will be safe while they relax, do their shopping or go to work. These crèches are run by nursery nurses.

Children may be in the care of a nursery nurse for the whole day. When this happens, the nursery nurse plans their day to include different types of activities, plus rests and meals.

Nursery nurses are trained to look after young babies.

Maria Montessori

Maria Montessori lived in Italy from 1870 to 1952. She worked with children with mental disabilities and from these experiences developed the Montessori method of nursery education.

She based this on the belief that young children should be taught in an informal way. She was sure that children can learn a great deal through play and should be allowed to develop at their own pace. The Montessori method still forms a basic part of some nursery education today.

Other children attend nurseries for just a few hours in the morning or afternoon, to help them grow used to mixing with groups of children and to prepare them for school.

Nursery nurses working in crèches in shopping centres or hotels do not usually have regular contact with the same children, but they still have to make their stay enjoyable by making sure they have interesting things to do.

Maria Montessori believed that children learn directly from their environment.

Main tasks of a nursery nurse

The main task of a nursery nurse is to provide a happy, safe environment where children can play and learn. They look after children in a practical way, making sure they are clean, they eat healthy, balanced meals and have a rest when necessary.

Very young children learn a great deal through play and nursery nurses have to make sure that activities are well planned to help children develop new skills, and to have fun.

Nursery nurses help children to develop:

- Social skills – learning to play with other children and to deal with the world outside their home.
- Practical skills – mastering tasks such as feeding and dressing themselves.
- Creative skills – expressing themselves through drawing, painting, music and dancing.
- Intellectual skills – naming colours, learning numbers and letters.
- Emotional skills – growing in confidence and making friends with other children.

Learning to feed yourself is a big step forward.

Good points and bad points

'The best part of my job is seeing children develop and learn new skills.'

'I do sometimes get very tired, because young children have a lot of energy and looking after them can be hard work.'

Nurses read to the children.

They also take the children on outside activities such as walks to parks and visits to shops, and arrange for outside visitors to come and talk to the children in the nursery.

As well as carrying out activities with groups of children, nursery nurses have to get to know every child in their group as an individual and help them with any problems they face.

They also have to keep up-to-date records of all the children in the nursery, containing information about their development, health and progress. These records are used when working out education programmes for each child.

Nursery nurses work as part of a team with parents, teachers, **social workers**, child psychologists (see pages 12-19) and family doctors.

Skills needed to be a nursery nurse

Enthusiasm and energy
Nursery nurses need to be bright and lively with lots
of imaginative ideas for activities to keep children
busy and happy.

Firmness
Nursery nurses must be fair but firm because young
children need gentle discipline to help them to learn
what is right and what is wrong.

Quick thinking
Dangerous situations can develop very quickly with
young children. A child may suddenly fall over, choke
on a piece of fruit, or try to run away from a group on
a walk. Nursery nurses need to be quick thinkers able
to deal swiftly and calmly with any situation.

First aid
Knowledge of **first aid** is important as accidents do
happen, however careful and watchful staff may be.
Staff have to be able to treat cuts and bruises and know
how to cope with children choking on food, swallowing
small objects or developing a sudden illness.

A trip to the park
is exciting and a
chance to learn
about flowers
and trees.

Health and safety

There are health and safety laws to make sure places where children spend their time are clean and secure. Nursery nurses have to know and keep these laws. For example, fire exits must not be blocked, toys must be safe to use, and equipment checked regularly and kept in good condition.

fact file

Nursery nurses need a recognised qualification in child care. Training includes time spent in college and work experience in different placements.

Play is an important part of a young child's development.

Understanding

Sometimes children are worried by problems, either at home or in the nursery. It is important for nursery nurses to recognise children who are unhappy or frightened. In some cases they may need to bring in more professional help, such as **social workers** or child psychologists (pages 12-19).

weblinks

For more information on the qualifications needed, go to www.waylinks.co.uk/series/soyouwant/children

A day in the life of a nursery nurse

Stephen Lynch

Stephen is a senior nursery nurse in a day nursery. He works in the toddler room with children aged between two and three years. The early shift is 7.00 am to 3.45 pm. The late shift is 9.30 am to 6.15 pm.

7.00 am This week I'm on the early shift and open up. I carry out safety checks and make sure there are no cleaning materials left out and no furniture or toys are broken. Then I sort out laundry and check the answer phone. Most children arrive between 8.30 and 9.00 am.

8.30 am We play with the children and make sure they're settled.

9.00 am Time to tidy up and encourage the children to put their toys away.

9.30 am Everyone has fruit and milk.

9.45 am I clear away while the children listen to a story. Some are toilet trained and need to be taken to the toilet regularly while others are still in nappies and need changing.

10.00 am A focused activity. At the moment we're looking at dinosaurs and the children are making dinosaur models from boxes and cartons.

11.45 am Lunchtime. Sometimes I eat lunch with the children, but today I have shopping to do.

12.30 pm I tidy the room and help to settle the children on sleeping mats. Some sleep for two hours and others for 20 minutes. We talk to parents or carers about children's sleep patterns and try to keep to the same routine.

1.30 pm   The children who are awake play with different toys. I try to keep the noise down so those who are still asleep are not disturbed.

2.30 pm   Everyone is up and ready for some fresh air so we take them outside for games, followed by a drink and circle time, when we all sit down for a chat.

3.45 pm   I tidy the kitchen before handing over to the late shift staff.

Time to go outside for some fresh air.

Very young children need a quiet time or a sleep during the day.

Child Psychologist

What is a child psychologist?

Child psychologists are highly qualified people, who are trained to help children deal with serious problems. These may be:

- learning and developmental problems – failure to grow, learn new skills and keep up with other children of the same age;
- behaviour and emotional problems – children can appear to be naughty or behave strangely when there is something wrong in their lives and they are feeling worried, angry or unhappy.

Child psychologists can work directly with children, meeting them regularly for one-to-one sessions.

They also meet children for assessment sessions to decide what is wrong. Then, working together with other professionals such as teachers (pages 52-59), nursery nurses (pages 4-11), doctors and **social workers**, they help to draw up a programme of support for the child. For example, children who dislike school and are absent a great deal can be encouraged to attend

Keeping up with new research is an important part of a child psychologist's work.

Looking at how children learn

As well as working with children who have problems, some child psychologists look into ways to help all children. For example, they carry out research into how children learn and use this information to develop teaching materials.

Over the years child psychologists have discovered a great deal about how children learn to read. This has led to the development of different methods of teaching.

through a programme which includes going to school for a short period of time each day, and having a teacher or carer who talks to them regularly about how school is going.

Child psychologists work in schools, **children's clinics** and hospitals. Some are self-employed and work in a **private practice** as **consultants** to different organizations and to private families.

Time spent with a child psychologist needs to be fun.

Helping children to deal with difficulties is a very skilled job and help is often needed over a long period. Child psychologists need to be very interested in how the human mind works and how children develop. Throughout their working life they must keep up with new developments and research.

Main tasks of a child psychologist

Child psychologists spend a lot of time talking to children and listening carefully to what they say. They watch them playing with toys and with other children at school or nursery and at home, in order to see for themselves how they behave and what skills they have.

They talk to adults who know the children well, such as parents or carers, nursery nurses (pages 4-11) and teachers (pages 52-9), to build up a picture of the child's background and the problems they may be facing. They also give the children tasks or tests to do so they can measure what they can and cannot do.

When child psychologists have got to know a child very well and can understand the problems they are facing, they draw up a programme to help them.

Child psychologists can help families to deal with their problems.

Good points and bad points

'It is very rewarding to work with other people, helping children overcome problems. However there are times when I see my advice ignored and this can be frustrating.'

A child carrying out some psychological tests.

For example, children who become angry and hurt themselves and other children, can be helped with **anger management programmes**. These involve helping the children to realise what is happening and how to deal with their feelings before they explode into a temper tantrum. The programme would also include training adults to recognise early signs of a possible incident and to help the children to deal with it without becoming violent.

Child psychologists' work includes sharing information and giving advice on how best to help children. All the adults involved with helping the child make decisions about the child's future together. This might involve:

- extra support in school or nursery;
- **therapy sessions**;
- a place at a school or unit run by specially trained staff.

Work with a child can go on for several years and child psychologists take part in regular reviews. Here they consider how a child is progressing and whether the help they are receiving is still right for them.

Skills needed to be a child psychologist

Observation
Child psychologists need to be very observant and able to pick up on very small clues which may help them to understand what is troubling a child.

Analysis
An important part of a child psychologist's work involves examining reports about children's behaviour, and lifting information from them. The ability to examine and analyse information is vital.

Flexibility
All children are different and child psychologists need to be flexible in the way they work and be prepared to think of different ways of helping their patients. They also need to be friendly and put children at ease.

A great deal can be learned from watching children at play.

Patience
Helping children can be a slow business and so a lot of patience is needed to deal with the long periods of time when there does not seem to be a great deal of progress.

Emotional strength
Working with children with problems can be distressing and child psychologists need to cope with sad and difficult situations.

Report writing is part of a child psychologist's job.

Communication

Child psychologists must explain things clearly and simply to children and to the adults caring for them and working with them.

Teamwork

Child psychologists need to enjoy working as part of a team with parents, carers, teachers, doctors and nurses.

Organisation

They have to be well organised and deal with a great deal of paperwork which can include writing long reports about patients.

fact file

Psychologists need a university degree in psychology before they can begin professional training.

Educational psychologists specialise in work with children in schools. They first train as teachers and spend several years working with children and young people, before taking a year's further training in psychology. The next year is spent working under the supervision and guidance of experienced educational psychologists.

A day in the life of a child psychologist

Fiona McKendrick

Fiona is a child psychologist. She works with children who have been referred to her by other professionals who are concerned about the child's development. Fiona has a **first degree** in sociology with psychology and a **master's degree** in clinical psychology.

8.45 am The day begins with a team meeting when staff discuss the children who have appointments that day.

9.30 am The centre runs an assessment nursery. This is where pre-school children come for sessions with one or two other children, so staff can observe them while they play.

The next two hours are spent in the nursery playing with the children, observing them and finding out information from parents or carers.

12.00 pm A feedback session with parents about the session in the nursery. Decisions on a child's future are made in discussion with other professionals.

12.45 pm I leave the centre for a home visit to see a child who has eating problems. I make sure I'm there at a meal time, and have a chat with his mother about ways to encourage him to eat.

2.15 pm A **family therapy** session based around social skills training for an autistic child. Autism is a development disorder, which affects a person's social and communication skills and their imagination.

3.45 pm   A school visit to talk over reports on a couple of pupils with their teachers and to discuss with them ways of helping the pupils to deal with their difficulties.

5.00 pm   I take some paperwork home with me to check during the evening.

A chance to exchange ideas and information with another professional.

Helping children to cope with difficulties can be very rewarding.

weblinks

For more information on a career in psychology, go to www.waylinks.co.uk/ series/soyouwant/children

Child Therapist

What is a child therapist?

Child therapists use different activities to help children overcome problems or cope with disabilities. They work both one-to-one with a child and with groups of children with similar problems.

They work in hospitals, clinics, schools, nurseries and health centres and visit children in their own homes. Some child therapists are **self-employed** and work for a number of different organizations.

Some therapists work with children to overcome particular problems caused by ill health, physical and mental disability, accidents or medical treatment. For example:

- Speech therapists work with children who have problems with speech and language. This could be because of physical problems such as hearing or the way their mouth and tongue are formed. Lack of speech can also be a sign of emotional problems.
- Physiotherapists help children to develop the use of their bodies and to regain physical movement after accidents or operations.

Exercising limbs is important after an accident or operation.

The history of therapy

There is nothing new in using pleasant activities to help people feel better about themselves and enjoy their lives. The Ancient Greeks, who lived 800-600 BC, realised the benefits of drama and used it to help people deal with mental health problems.

Children often find it hard to understand difficult events in their lives such as the death of a relative or their parents getting divorced. They can become too confused and worried to talk to adults about what is wrong. Therapists are trained to gain children's confidence and to help them express how they feel and come to terms with these events.

Making music is not only fun, it can be a way of finding strength to deal with problems.

There are many different methods or therapies, which are used to help children develop new skills or deal with problems. For example, play therapists use different types of games and play activities to help children, while other therapists specialise in a particular type of activity, such as:

● art;
● music;
● drama.

weblinks

For some images of music therapy at work, go to www.waylinks.co.uk/series/soyouwant/children

Main tasks of a child therapist

There are many ways in which therapists help children. For some children therapy is needed for just a short time to help them cope with an operation or a stay in hospital. For others who are coming to terms with a tragedy, such as the loss of a relation, or who are deeply troubled by a serious family problem, therapy can go on for months or even years.

Whatever the type of therapy, child therapists use their skills to help children individually. When working with a group, they have to be aware of the needs of each person. The way child therapists work with each patient varies enormously. There is no single way of helping children.

Working with others is an important part of drama therapy.

- Play therapists use dolls and toys to help children act out problems. In hospitals they calm worried children. They explain what is going to happen by using toy medical equipment, so the children are not frightened when they face the real thing.

Good points and bad points

'Music sessions can be great fun and I enjoy seeing children being creative. However, I do need a lot of patience because it takes a long time to win someone's trust.'

Art therapists
use different art
activities to help
children.

- Drama therapists use acting as a way of helping children to work and play as part of a group, developing their imagination and creative ability and helping them to move forward in a positive way.

- Music therapists encourage children to enjoy music and to use it to help them relax and to overcome difficult situations and problems. Therapy includes listening to music, singing and using different instruments to make music.

- Art therapists use all sorts of activities including model making, clay work and painting in their work with children. Art can be a good way of expressing things which are too difficult to put into words.

Skills needed to be a child therapist

Enthusiasm
Child therapists need to be enthusiastic and energetic about their work, in order to encourage patients to have fun and join in different activities.

Listening
They have to be able to win children's confidence and make them feel safe and secure. They also need good listening skills to be able to help and encourage children to talk about things that matter to them.

Imagination
No two children are the same and so no single programme will suit everyone. Child therapists need to be imaginative and able to develop new ideas for activities and to adapt programmes to suit individual children.

Listening carefully is an important skill for a child therapist.

Emotional strength
The strength to deal with sad and difficult situations is important because children need to be able to come to terms with their experiences and this can be very painful.

Patience
There is no quick way to help children. Progress can be slow and the work can be very demanding, so a

great deal of patience is needed. Child therapists have to remain positive at all times.

Organization
Child therapists need to be well organised because they work with a number of different patients and groups and may be required to travel from place to place. They need to keep records of activities and progress and to attend meetings with other professionals to discuss how children may be helped and to look at the progress they are making.

fact file

Physiotherapists and speech therapists are university graduates with bachelor's or master's degrees in physiotherapy or speech therapy. Courses include time spent working with patients in different settings such as hospitals, schools and nurseries. Art, music, drama and play therapists need a degree or a similar qualification in art, music or drama, plus experience of working with children or adults with problems, before being accepted for training as therapists.

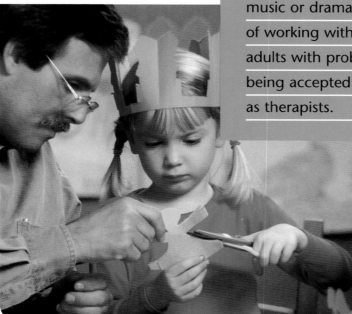

With help, everyone can enjoy being creative.

A day in the life of a child therapist

Alison Webster

Alison is a hospital play specialist in charge of a team of 14 play specialists in two hospitals. She is a qualified drama therapist and has a **master's degree** in play therapy.

8.30 am   I spend time writing letters and reports, before going on to the wards to see my team of play specialists.

10.00 am   A play session with children who are having surgery. I try to see things from the children's point of view and suggest to medical staff ways of making things easier for them.

The age group I work with ranges from babies to teenagers, some of them with **special needs**. My team and I also work with brothers and sisters of patients.

12.00 pm   A planning meeting with other hospital staff. We look at the list of children due to come into hospital and talk over ways we might help them.

I also help to organise pre-admission meetings when children come in to look around the hospital before they are admitted. This means there will be familiar faces to welcome them and their families or carers when they come in for treatment.

2.00 pm   After lunch I give a lecture to medical students training to be doctors, on how to use play to communicate with children. I stress to them that every child must be treated as an individual.

4.30 pm   A play therapy session with a girl who has diabetes and is refusing to take her medication regularly. Together we decide what is important for me to talk about to her family, nurses and doctors, without telling them anything she has told me, which is private between us. I try to help them understand how she is feeling.

Play therapy can include different kinds of activities.

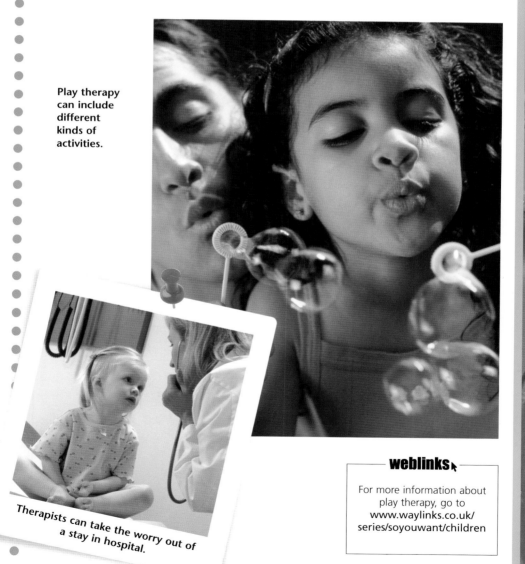

Therapists can take the worry out of a stay in hospital.

weblinks

For more information about play therapy, go to www.waylinks.co.uk/ series/soyouwant/children

Paediatrician

What is a paediatrician?

Paediatricians are doctors of medicine who specialise in the care of children aged from birth to 16 years. They train as doctors at university or medical school and then take further qualifications in paediatrics (child health).

Children see paediatricians for a number of different reasons:

- Their family doctor is not sure exactly what is wrong and wants further tests or investigations to be carried out by someone with specialist knowledge.
- The treatment that a child needs is too complicated to be carried out by the family doctor and needs to be done by a paediatrician in a hospital.
- Children have a disability or a condition such as diabetes which needs to be controlled throughout their lives. They are registered with a paediatrician and attend the hospital for regular visits throughout their childhood. When they become adults they are transferred to another **consultant**.

The work of a paediatrician begins at birth.

A world health success story

Paediatricians are concerned with raising the health standards of all children. One big success story in child health is the stamping out of **smallpox** across the world.

In 1967 the **World Health Organisation** started a campaign to vaccinate the world's children against smallpox and the last recorded case of the disease was in 1978.

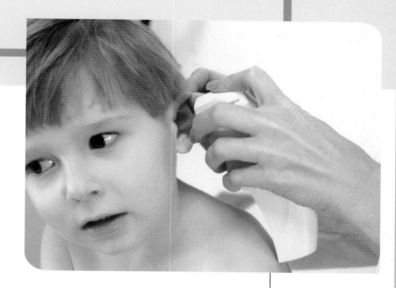

Paediatricians are part of a team of medical staff caring for sick children.

Most paediatricians are attached to hospitals and see their patients there. They see them:

- in **outpatients** departments, where patients visit the hospital for an appointment, but do not stay overnight.
- in children's wards, where patients stay when they are receiving on-going treatment or are having surgery.

weblinks

For more information on the duties of a paediatrician, go to
www.waylinks.co.uk/
series/soyouwant/children

Main tasks of a paediatrician

The work of paediatricians is similar to that of other doctors. The difference is that all their patients are children.

Newborn babies may be seen by a paediatrician because medical staff are concerned for their health or development. Otherwise, the first contact with a paediatrician is usually when a child visits the hospital for an outpatient appointment. The paediatricians carry out investigations and tests to find out what is wrong and then decide on suitable treatment.

Sometimes this means the child goes into hospital for further tests, for medical treatment, or for a surgical operation. In other cases the paediatrician can suggest treatment which is carried out by the family doctor.

It is important to make sure a child is growing normally.

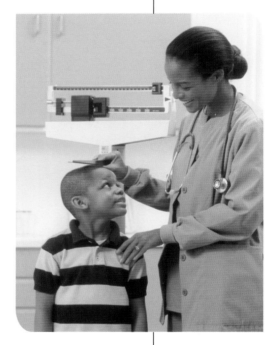

Good points and bad points

'When a child is ill or in pain, it can be very difficult to treat them. At the same time dealing with their relatives and carers is also hard, because they are so upset and worried.'

'The good part is seeing children recover and enjoy life again.'

It is not easy to find out (diagnose) what is wrong with children, especially when they are too young to talk or to understand what is happening. As well as examining the patient very carefully, paediatricians spend a long time talking to parents and carers to try and find out what is wrong.

When paediatricians see patients they send a report of their findings to family doctors, so they are kept informed of what is going on. They also work closely with other hospital staff such as nurses, physiotherapists (see page 20) and **radiographers** and **radiologists** in x-ray departments.

Many different staff are involved in the care of sick children and records need to be kept up-to-date so everyone involved knows what is happening.

Children in hospital receive regular visits from their paediatrician.

Skills needed to be a paediatrician

Observation
Babies and young children cannot explain what is wrong and this can make diagnosing their problems difficult. Paediatricians need to be very observant and notice even the smallest changes in their patients.

Patience
They need a great deal of patience because sick children are often frightened and are easily upset. This means examinations and treatment have to be taken slowly with the patients being given a lot of comfort and reassurance.

A gentle touch
A gentle but sure touch is needed so children suffer as little as possible when receiving treatment. Paediatricians need to be very good at using their hands because children's bodies are smaller than those of adults and this can make carrying out tasks such as giving injections very difficult.

Paediatricians need to gain the trust of their patients and their parents or carers.

Emotional strength
Emotional strength is important because looking after sick children can be hard. Not all patients get better and paediatricians have to accept this and still give the best care possible.

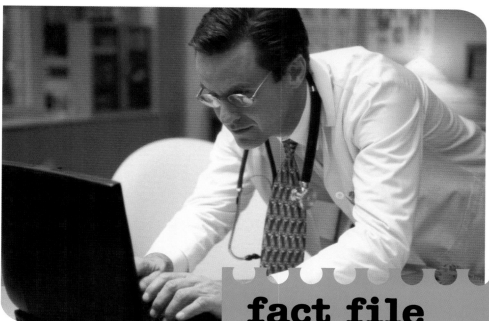

Records have to be kept up-to-date.

Communication skills

A lot of time is spent talking to patients, to parents and carers as well as to other medical staff. Paediatricians need to be able to explain quite complicated facts clearly and simply in a way that can be understood by people who do not have a lot of medical knowledge.

fact file

Paediatricians first train as doctors which takes around five years at medical school. After finishing this general training they take further training in paediatrics. It can take between four and six more years for a doctor to be registered as a specialist paediatrician.

Teamwork

Paediatricians need to enjoy working as part of a team because keeping children healthy and making sick children well involves more than one person.

A day in the life of a paediatrician

Anna Livermore

Anna is a paediatrician. She trained as a doctor and then gained a further qualification in paediatrics.

9.00 am   The day starts with a ward round. There are around 25 beds in the ward and the round takes about two hours.

Most of the patients are medical cases which means they are in hospital for treatment, not operations, but we do deal with emergency surgical cases.

11.00 am   The **consultants**, nurses and **junior doctors** meet to discuss patients.

11.30 am   Back on the ward, I organise **scans** and x-rays, replace **drips** and carry out other procedures.

I try to find time to make phone calls to other professionals involved with the patients, such as physiotherapists (see page 20), **occupational therapists**, **social workers** and family doctors.

2.00 pm   I have an **outpatients'** clinic where I see children referred to the hospital by family doctors. Quite a number of them have respiratory (breathing) complaints such as asthma.

Tending patients takes up a large part of the day and sometimes the night.

Interpreting an x-ray is not always straightforward.

The hospital is not large enough to have specialist paediatricians who work in particular areas of paediatrics. This means I see a wide range of conditions at outpatients' stage. If a patient has a problem which is likely to need surgery, I refer them to a surgeon.

Most surgeons treat both adults and children, so for example, I would send a child suffering from a hip pain to an **orthopaedic surgeon**.

4.30 pm   A chance to dictate some letters.

If I'm on call for the night I remain in the hospital. As well as covering the children's wards, on-call paediatricians cover the special care baby unit where sick and **premature babies** are cared for. This means the nights are always very busy.

Paediatric Nurse

What is a paediatric nurse?

Paediatric nurses are qualified, **registered** medical nurses who have taken extra training in order to work with sick children aged between birth and 16 years.

They work in **medical centres** and in doctors' practices and on children's wards in hospitals. Some work on **intensive care** wards, nursing very seriously ill children. Others work in **hospices** caring for sick children who are not going to recover from their illness. Paediatric nurses also work in the community, visiting sick children in their own homes to give them treatment and to advise parents and carers on looking after them.

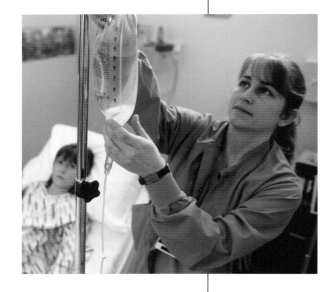

Sick children need specialist nursing care.

As well as working with children who are sick, paediatric nurses work with children who have physical and mental disabilities.

To do this type of work paediatric nurses need to be very interested in child health. New developments in medicine are always taking place and they have to keep up-to-date with these changes.

The battle against malaria

Paediatric nurses, especially those working in the developing world, help to educate people on health issues.

In parts of Africa, malaria is a serious problem. The disease is spread through the bite of a certain type of mosquito and it causes many deaths every year, especially in areas where food is scarce.

Programmes are in place to tackle malaria, using drugs and educating people to sleep under mosquito nets.

Paediatric nurses help children to feel settled and comfortable in hospital.

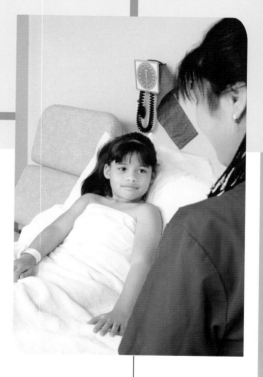

It is important to have nurses specialising in the care of children because children's bodies, unlike those of adults, are still growing and developing and this process can be affected by illness or injury.

Some illnesses such as **croup** are more likely to affect children than adults and paediatric nurses need experience in dealing with these.

Children, especially when they are very young, can develop serious illnesses quickly and become extremely sick and in need of specialist nursing care in a short space of time.

Main tasks of a paediatric nurse

Paediatric nurses work closely with other members of the medical team including doctors, nurses and therapists. They have a great deal of contact with the sick children and play a major role in helping them recover from illness or surgery and return to health.

While adult patients are able to understand what is happening and why they are in need of treatment, children, especially those who are very young, have little idea of what is going on.

Nurses work as part of a team, supporting the patients and their relatives.

They feel ill and are often frightened by the treatment they receive. Injections and anaesthetics can be terrifying, and paediatric nurses have to carry out these tasks calmly and professionally. Nurses comfort the patients and help them to understand as far as possible what is happening to them.

Good points and bad points

'Helping children to get well is really rewarding.'

'The difficult part of my job is accepting that not all my patients will recover.'

The work of a paediatric nurse includes:

- Giving patients medicines and injections.
- Cleaning wounds and changing dressings and bandages.
- Taking out stitches when wounds have healed.
- Taking blood samples from patients and sending them to laboratories to be analysed.
- Taking patients' pulse and temperature.
- Keeping records of patients, to make sure that other staff are fully aware of their condition and progress.
- Getting to know the patients, giving them support, playing with them and with those who are old enough to understand, explaining to them what is happening.
- Discussing patients' progress with their relations and carers and helping them to cope with the distress they feel.

Dressings and bandages need to be changed regularly.

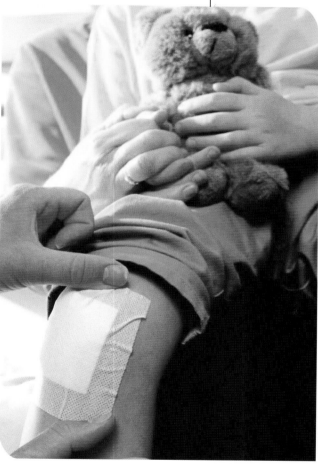

weblinks

For more information about children's nursing in the NHS, go to www.waylinks.co.uk/ series/soyouwant/children

Skills needed to be a paediatric nurse

A positive outlook

A positive outlook is needed, and this is not always easy because paediatric nurses deal with some sad and distressing cases. They need to be strong enough to cope with these, and to support patients and their families and carers. Then they have to move on to help their next patient.

A calm approach

A cool head and a calm approach to all situations are vital because emergencies do occur when nursing sick children. These have to be dealt with quickly and efficiently if lives are to be saved.

Tact

Paediatric nurses need to be reassuring, tactful and patient in order to calm patients and their families and win their confidence. It is distressing for everyone when children are ill and paediatric nurses play a big part in helping people to cope.

Strong stomach

Illness is a dirty business and paediatric nurses need strong stomachs in order to cope with blood, vomit and mess.

Some patients can get up and play while others have to stay in bed.

Gentle hands

Some of the treatments such as giving injections and putting in feeding tubes are very difficult to perform on babies and small children. Paediatric nurses need to be good with their hands, so they cause as little pain to patients as possible.

Paediatric nurses work shifts to provide care throughout the day and night.

fact file

Paediatric nurses first train as general nurses in hospitals. This usually takes around three years. It is also possible to go to university and take a degree in nursing. The next step for a paediatric nurse is to take further training and to work with sick children while being supervised (guided and helped) by experienced medical staff.

Communication skills

Good communication skills are important, both speaking and writing. Paediatric nurses have to write reports on children's treatment and progress and explain situations clearly to other medical staff, patients and their families and carers.

A day in the life of a paediatric nurse

Ben Stevens

Ben is a paediatric nurse, running a paediatric **surgical** ward. He works a four day week, involving two twelve and a half hour **clinical days** spent on the ward, and two eight hour office days dealing with paperwork.

7.30 am   It's a clinical day and I arrive on the ward.

7.45 am   Handover, when the day staff are briefed by the night staff on events during their shift.

I allocate patients to nurses. Each nurse has a bedside handover with the night nurse caring for his or her patients.

8.00 am   I go round the ward checking patients' charts and medication and talking to parents. We have premature babies with a minimum weight of 1.6 kilos and many parents or carers stay in the ward with their children.

8.45 am   There are four paediatric surgeons on the ward and I try to accompany them on their rounds. If a patient's nurse is not present I pass on information to them.

10.00 am   I organise coffee breaks and arrange cover for staff involved in **one-to-one nursing**. This is followed by a quick ward round.

Throughout the day physiotherapists (see page 20), **dieticians** and other staff visit patients and I brief them on their progress.

12.00 pm   One afternoon a week I attend a bed meeting when medical staff discuss patients coming in the following week. On another afternoon there's a psycho-social meeting attended by myself, social workers and play specialists where we discuss the social needs of patients and their families.

4.00 pm   If there's a quiet time of the day it's around now.

5.00 pm   The paediatric surgeons do their evening rounds.

7.00 pm   I prepare for the arrival of the night staff, updating and printing out the handover sheet.

7.45 pm   Handover has finished and it's time to go home.

Details of treatment and progress need to be recorded with care.

Nurses and doctors work closely together to give the best possible care.

Nursery Teacher

What is a nursery teacher?

Nursery teachers work with children who are not yet old enough to attend school, but who are ready to start preparing for the lessons they will learn when they get there.

Nursery teachers work in private nurseries and in nursery classes attached to schools. Some nursery education is provided free of charge by the local education authority and some is privately run, which means parents pay fees to send their children to classes.

Nursery teachers are responsible for drawing up educational programmes. Together with other staff they decide on topics to be covered during the term, linking activities to different themes such as the zoo, the circus, Autumn and Spring.

Nursery teachers make learning fun.

One of the most important tasks of nursery teachers and their staff is to prepare children for school so they settle down quickly and are not worried or frightened by being in the classroom. They also prepare children

The first nursery school

Friedrich Froebel lived in Germany between 1782 and 1852. He wrote a book called *Education of Man* in which he set out his ideas about education through play. In 1836 he opened the first nursery school.

Friedrich Froebel believed that children as young as three years were capable of learning and he trained teachers in his nursery so they could open other nurseries based on his ideas.

for learning by teaching them to recognise numbers, letters, shapes and colours.

They usually work with older children in the year or 18 months before they start school. By this age the children have gained the social skills they will need in school and are able to talk, feed and dress themselves.

Nursery teachers arrange all sorts of activities.

The children are still very young and find it difficult to do any activity for very long. Learning is mostly through play, for example learning numbers by singing counting and action songs.

Main tasks of a nursery teacher

Nursery teachers help children to enjoy learning and to prepare for school. To do this they work not only with pupils, but with their parents or carers and form strong links between nursery and home. They get to know all the children in their care as individuals, and work out learning programmes for each one of them, taking into account their age, character and ability.

Teachers work as part of a team.

Good points and bad points

'The children I teach are at a lovely age and I enjoy being with them.'

'My job is hectic and I often find I run out of time for all the jobs I have to do.'

They design and make learning materials such as
number cards and word cards to help pupils to learn.
They arrange for visitors such as members of the
police or firemen to come to the nursery and talk to
the children about their work and to advise them
about keeping safe.

They measure the progress of each child and keep
records to show their development.

Nursery teachers work as part of a team of
professionals including nursery nurses (pages 4-12)
and speech therapists (page 20) to make sure children
are happy and settled and are progressing well. They
also plan and organise the work of **classroom
assistants** and helpers.

Working closely with school staff, nursery teachers try
to make sure the move from nursery school to school
goes as smoothly as possible for every child. This
could include organising visits to the new school and
having school staff visit the nursery.

Skills needed to be a nursery teacher

Friendliness
They need to have a calm, friendly manner so the children feel relaxed and comfortable with them. Children who are worried or frightened find it very difficult to learn.

Discipline
A firm but kind approach is important because gentle but regular discipline is needed to create an atmosphere in which children feel secure and are able to learn.

Teachers need to have a good relationship with children and their parents or carers.

Enthusiasm
Nursery teachers need a lively personality and enthusiasm for their work, so they can make learning fun for their pupils.

Communication
Good communication skills are important because nursery teachers need to explain things in a clear, simple way to pupils. They also need to talk to parents and carers. Tact is needed when teachers discuss a child's difficulties with parents or carers.

Quick thinking
Nursery teachers have to think quickly and be able to deal with any situation that arises. If a child becomes ill or has an accident in class, or is angry with another child, they need to step in and deal with the situation immediately.

Children need praise and encouragement if they are to do well.

fact file

Nursery teachers can take a degree in primary education, or a degree in any subject followed by a teacher training course.

Teamwork

Nursery teachers have to enjoy working as part of a team, which includes nursery nurses (pages 4-12), therapists (pages 20-27), parents and carers.

Organisation

There is a lot of paperwork and record keeping involved in teaching, and nursery teachers need to be well organised and keep up-to-date records.

Claire Aylward

Claire is a nursery teacher in a private nursery. She has a degree in psychology and a teaching qualification.

9.15 am I'm on late shift, so the children are in when I arrive and I have a quick briefing with staff.

I work with three to five year olds and I'm responsible for planning activities. We have a long term plan covering the year. Every week I work out a detailed plan, covering what staff will do and what equipment will be used.

9.30 am Fruit and drinks are put out and the children help themselves.

10.00 am A chance to talk about our present topic – farming, with the children. At their suggestion we've put potatoes and carrots in the sandpit to turn it into a field.

Throughout the day I observe the children and make notes of what they can do. We have a daily maths activity and follow the same learning to read programme as the local schools which our children will attend. But learning is largely through play.

10.30 am Focused activities such as cooking, or gardening.

We have a **free flow system** where we discuss focused activities with the children and they decide what they want to do. Focused activities are those which the children do with direct help from a member of staff.

11.00 am	Unless it's raining we go outside for games.
11.30 am	Lunch. The children sit in small groups and help themselves to food.
12.15 pm	Time for free play, which for some children is singing and playing musical instruments.
1.45 pm	Focused activities.
3.30 pm	Teatime.
4.00 pm	The day is beginning to wind down, with table top activities and story tapes.
5.30 pm	Most of the children have been collected, and there's a chance to talk over the day's activities and think about tomorrow.

Learning numbers can be part of a game.

Playing musical instruments is all part of learning.

weblinks

For more case studies, go to
www.waylinks.co.uk/
series/soyouwant/children

Schoolteacher

What is a schoolteacher?

A teacher is responsible for educating children. With very young children their main task is teaching them to master the basic skills of reading, writing and working with numbers, although they would also teach them other subjects such as geography and science.

A teacher has to teach a large number of children at one time.

There's nothing new about exams!

Pupils have been taking exams for a very long time. In Ancient China, examinations were set for candidates wanting to work in administrative posts for the government. The examinations tested their knowledge of Chinese literature. Those who gained the highest marks got the jobs.

Usually teachers work with a particular age group:
Pupils aged up to 10 or 11 years (primary);
Pupils aged 11 to 18 years (secondary);
Sixth formers aged 16 to 18 years.

Teachers working with children aged around 11 years old or under, are usually class teachers and take the same class or group of children for almost all their lessons.

Working in a group can be a good way to learn.

Once children move to high schools, upper schools or secondary schools, the system changes. Lessons are taught by specialist teachers, who teach one or maybe two subjects to different classes throughout the school.

In addition to teaching, many teachers also have a pastoral or caring role. They are responsible for a form or class and make sure that the pupils in their class are in school and working well. If pupils have a problem the class teacher is there to help them.

Main tasks of a schoolteacher

Teachers spend a large part of their day in the classroom, giving lessons to pupils.

These lessons don't just happen. Teachers spend a great deal of time planning them, making sure they are interesting and that all the pupils in the class have work to match their ability.

Marking pupils' work is important because it helps teachers to see what children do or do not understand. Reading a teacher's comment on their work encourages pupils to do well.

Pupils need a lot of encouragement, which is why teachers discuss their progress with them and do their best to help them with any problems they may be having. They also keep up-to-date records of pupils' progress and achievement and write reports to be sent to parents and carers.

Teachers meet together to discuss how the school is to be organised.

Good points and bad points

'I love being with the children, but I do find the paperwork can be a problem. There are always forms and reports to fill in and with all my other work I find it difficult to get paperwork done.'

Schools organise regular meetings between teachers and parents and carers, so they can work together to help pupils enjoy school and make progress. These meetings are often held in the evening or after school. Teachers make themselves available to see parents or carers who want to come in to school to talk about a particular matter.

Most schools organise activities such as drama, art, music or sport for pupils, which are run by teachers.

During lunch and break times, teachers may be on duty, walking around the school and making sure pupils are well behaved.

In their free time teachers have to keep up with new developments in their subjects and with changes in the way lessons are being taught and schools are being run.

It might seem at first that the hours teachers work are quite short, but the time spent in the classroom is only one part of their work. Most teachers put in many hours a week preparing lessons, writing and designing work sheets for pupils to use, and marking the work they have done.

Many teachers run sport and leisure clubs for pupils.

Skills needed to be a schoolteacher

Respect
In order to teach, a person needs to like and respect children, whatever their background or ability, and must be able to treat all pupils fairly.

Good explanation skills
Teachers not only need a good understanding of the subjects they teach, they also need to be able to explain things in a way which is simple and easy to understand.

Interesting, lively approach
An interesting, lively approach is needed by teachers because pupils learn best when they find lessons exciting, stimulating and informative.

There are a great many ways to make a lesson interesting.

Patience
It is not always easy to teach a class of children, with different ideas and abilities. Being a teacher demands a great deal of patience.

Discipline
A firm but fair approach to discipline is needed. Pupils need to behave properly because a calm atmosphere is needed in the classroom if children are to be able to concentrate on their work.

Organization
There is a lot of official paperwork for teachers to fill in about the lessons they have given and the progress

Talking over a problem is often the first step to solving it.

fact file

To become a teacher you need to gain a university degree which includes a teaching qualification as part of the course. Alternatively, you can take a degree in any subject, and then take a teacher training course.

made by their pupils. Regular meetings with parents and carers and other members of staff form part of a teacher's work. Teachers need to be very well organised in order to cope with busy working lives.

Teamwork

Teachers need to like people of all ages and to get on well with them. They need to enjoy working as part of a team, which includes colleagues and pupils, parents and carers.

weblinks

For more information about training and teaching, go to www.waylinks.co.uk/series/soyouwant/children

Phil Grainger

Phil teaches history in a secondary school.

8.15 am	I arrive and check my emails. News about lesson changes, special events and pupils is emailed out daily.
8.45 am	**Registration** with my class of 12 to 13 year olds. I check **lesson planners** and diaries in which pupils plan their work. I collect notes from parents, pass on messages, talk to pupils, and have a word with anyone who's in trouble.
9.05 am	A double lesson on ancient Greece with 11 year olds. We're looking at aspects of everyday life for the ancient Greeks – housing, education, medicine, games and leisure.
10.35 am	Break time. I might manage a coffee, but often spend time sorting out issues from previous classes.
10.55 am	A lesson with my registration class. They are writing comments about their school reports. I encourage them to look at developing their strengths and coping with their weaknesses.
11.40 am	A class of 16 year olds who are working on their coursework projects on the Second World War. I check up on their progress and answer any questions that have arisen along the way.
12.25 pm	My 18 year old pupils are preparing for various exam papers, including the Russian Revolution and the history of the USA. We cover several revision topics today.

1.10 pm   Lunchtime is only 45 minutes. I eat quickly, while sorting out problems and booking the minibus for a PE trip.

1.55 pm   I have a double lesson with a special needs group, who are finding work difficult. We may work on history, or I may help them with reading and writing skills.

3.25 pm   The pupils leave. My work doesn't end here though – I have plenty of marking and paperwork to get through before the next day.

History lesson in progress.

Once classes end it's time to tackle the marking.

Glossary

anaesthetic – medication given to send a patient to sleep, usually before an operation. It is often given in the form of an injection.

anger management programme – a list of activities drawn up to help someone to control his or her temper.

children's clinic – a medical centre specialising in children's health and development.

classroom assistant – a person who supports teachers by helping them with lessons. This could be supporting individual children who are having difficulties or doing practical jobs such as printing out work sheets.

clinical day – a day spent working on a hospital ward.

consultant – a senior doctor specialising in a particular area of medicine.

crèche – a place run by trained staff where parents or carers can leave their children to be looked after, while they go to work, do shopping, study or play a sport. Crèches are often attached to shopping centres, sports centres, colleges or work places.

croup – an inflammation of the throat and windpipe in children, causing a hard cough and difficulty in breathing.

day care centre – a place where children are looked after.

dietician – a trained professional who gives advice on what to eat; for example working out a meal plan for a child who has diabetes.

drip – a tube put into a part of a patient's body such as an arm or a leg, through which liquids needed by the patient are passed into the body.

family therapy – counselling help given to family groups instead of individuals.

first aid – emergency treatment given to a sick or injured person before trained medical help arrives.

first degree – the qualification usually called a bachelor's degree, taken by university undergraduates.

free flow system – a programme where children move around from activity to activity.

health visitor – a trained medical professional, usually a nurse who has taken additional qualifications and works with children in the community.

hospice – a hospital where people with incurable illnesses are treated. Hospices cannot make patients well but they treat their pain and make the last part of their lives as pleasant as possible.

intensive care – the nursing of patients who are very ill and need a high level of attention.

junior doctor – a recently qualified person working in a hospital while being supported and advised by more experienced medical staff.

lesson planner – programme of classroom activities.

master's degree – a second university qualification taken by students who have already gained a bachelor's degree.

medical centre – a place where doctors and nurses are based and where they see patients and carry out treatments.

nanny – a person who looks after small groups of children, usually in the same family.

nursery – a place where children under school age are cared for and taught.

occupational therapist – therapists who use selected activities to help patients restore, develop or maintain skills.

one-to-one nursing – individual care for a very sick patient.

orthopaedic surgeon – a medical consultant specialising in the treatment of bones.

outpatient – a person who visits a hospital to see a doctor or to receive treatment, but who doesn't stay overnight in a ward.

pastoral – means caring. A teacher who has a pastoral role not only teaches an academic subject but also helps pupils cope with personal difficulties.

play centre – a place where children can go and enjoy different activities.

premature babies – those born early, before the date they are due.

private practice – work carried out by doctors for which they are paid by the patient or the patient's medical insurance company.

radiographer – a technician trained to take x-rays.

radiologist – a doctor specially trained to understand and explain what is shown in an x-ray.

registered – enrolled or entered, for example on a doctor's list as a patient.

registration – the act of enrolling or entering yourself or another person for an activity or on a record.

scan – using different methods such as ultra-sound (sound vibrations) to make a picture of part of the body.

self-employed – working for yourself rather than for another person or organisation.

smallpox – a serious, often fatal disease which has now been wiped out. Sufferers had a high temperature and were covered with blisters.

social worker – a trained professional person who helps people with problems, for example children whose parents are unable to look after them, or elderly people who find it difficult to cope on their own.

special needs – people with special needs have handicaps or disabilities which mean they need extra support to live their lives as fully as possible.

surgical – a process involving an operation on a patient.

therapy sessions – set times when a person trained to help others overcome particular problems, works with an individual or a small group.

World Health Organisation – a section of the United Nations set up to prevent and wipe out diseases across the globe.

Further Information

So do you still want to work with children?

This book does not aim to cover every job that involves working with children, and many, including those of **health visitor**, **nanny**, and **social worker** are missing.

What it does hope to do is to give you an idea of the range of different jobs, and what working with children is really like.

It is natural to love children and to enjoy playing with them, but that is not the same as working with them all day, every day. To do that you need to be a special type of person. You need to be able to put yourself in the children's place and have an idea of how they feel, even when they are at their most difficult and demanding.

The way to find out if a job with children is right for you is to find out as much as you can about such work. When you are old enough you could think about doing voluntary work with a youth group or children's play group.

If you are at secondary school and seriously interested in a certain career, ask your careers teacher if he or she could arrange for some work experience. This means spending some time, usually a week or two, in an area of your chosen profession. In this instance, you could go to a **nursery**, a **crèche**, or to another setting with children.

Books

If you want to find out more about working with children, you will find the following helpful:

Careers Working With Children, written by Judith Humphries, published by Kogan Page, 2000.

Careers in Medicine, Dentistry and Mental Health, written by Loulou Brown, published by Kogan Page, 2000.

Working in Nursing, published by Connexions, 2001.

Working with Young Children, published by Connexions, 2002.

Working in Teaching, published by Connexions, 2001.

Leaflets are available from the Council for Awards in Children's Care and Education (see under Nursery Nurse addresses).

weblinks

For websites relevant to this book, go to
www.waylinks.co.uk/
series/soyouwant/children

Useful addresses

Nursery Nurse/Child Care Worker

Council for Awards in
Children's Care and
Education (CACHE)
8 Chequer Street
St Albans
Hertfordshire
AL1 3XZ
Tel: 01727 847636

National Training
Organisation for Early Years
Pilgrims Lodge
Holywell Hill
St Albans
AL1 1ER
Tel 01727 738300

Professional Association of
Nursery Nurses (PANN)
2 St James' Court
Friar Gate
Derby
DE1 1BT
Tel: 01332 372337

Child Psychologist/ Counsellor

The British Psychological
Society
St Andrew's House
48 Princess Road East
Leicester
LE1 7DR
Tel: 0116 254 9568

Child Therapist

Association of Professional
Music Therapists
26 Hamlyn Road
Glastonbury
BA6 8HT
Tel: 01458 834919

British Association of Art
Therapists
Mary Ward House
5 Tavistock Place
London
WC1H 9SN
Tel: 0207 383 3774

British Association of
Drama Therapists
41 Broomhouse Lane
London
SW6 3DP
Tel: 0207 731 0160

British Association of Play
Therapists
31 Cedar Drive
Keynsham
Bristol
BS31 2TY
Tel: 0117 986 0390

British Association of
Psychotherapists
37 Mapesbury Road
London
NW2 4HJ
Tel: 0208 452 9823

Chartered Society of
Physiotherapy
14 Bedford Row
London
WC1R 4ED
Tel: 0207 306 6666

College of Occupational
Therapists
106-114 Borough High Street
Southwark
London
SE1 1LB
Tel: 0207 357 6480

Royal College of Speech and
Language Therapists
2 White Hart Yard
London
SE1 1NX
Tel: 0207 378 1200

Paediatrician

British Medical Association
Tavistock Square
London
WC1H 9JP
Tel: 0207 387 4499

General Medical Council
178 Great Portland Street
London
W1W 5JE
Tel: 0207 580 7642

Paediatric Nurse/ Children's Nurse

NHS Careers
PO Box 376
Bristol
BS99 3EY
Tel: 0845 6060 655

Nursing and Midwifery
Council
23 Portland Place
London
W1B 1PZ
Tel: 0207 637 718

Nursery Teacher/ Pre-school Teacher

CACHE
(See under Nursery Nurse)

Schoolteacher

Teacher Training Agency
(TTA)
Portland House
Stag Place
London
SW1E 5TT
Tel: 0207 925 3700

Index